T0001185

GOD'S COSMIC COOKBOOK

YOUR COMPLETE GUIDE TO MAKING A UNIVERSE

ELIZABETH COLE

Illustrated by **PATRICK LAURENT**

First published in Great Britain in 2023 by Hodder & Stoughton
An Hachette UK company

Copyright © Elizabeth Cole 2023
Illustrations Copyright © Patrick Laurent 2023

The right of Elizabeth Cole to be identified as the Author of the Work has been asserted
by her in accordance with the Copyright, Designs and Patents Act 1988.

The right of Patrick Laurent to be identified as the Illustrator of the Work has been
asserted by him in accordance with the Copyright, Designs and Patents Act 1988.

Scripture quotations from *The Holy Bible, New International Version*® Copyright ©1973,
1978, 1984, 2011 by Biblica, Inc.® Used by permission. All rights reserved worldwide.

All rights reserved. No part of this publication may be reproduced, stored in a retrieval
system, or transmitted, in any form or by any means without the prior written permission
of the publisher, nor be otherwise circulated in any form of binding or cover other than
that in which it is published and without a similar condition being imposed on the
subsequent purchaser.

A CIP catalogue record for this title is available from the British Library

Trade Paperback ISBN 978 1 399 80648 0
eBook ISBN 978 1 399 80649 7

Printed and bound in Great Britain by Clays Ltd, Elcograf S.p.A.

Hodder & Stoughton policy is to use papers that are natural, renewable and recyclable
products and made from wood grown in sustainable forests. The logging and
manufacturing processes are expected to conform to the environmental regulations of
the country of origin.

Hodder & Stoughton Ltd
Carmelite House
50 Victoria Embankment
London EC4Y 0DZ

www.hodderfaithyoungexplorers.co.uk

CONTENTS

HELLO, and welcome to my Cosmic Cookbook – your handy step-by-step guide to creating life, a universe and everything – your introduction to the science of creating a cosmos and the creating of science itself!

It's all written out like one huge recipe so you can try it at home. It takes a lot longer than scrambling eggs, but it's much more exciting and the science is out of this world... it'll help you see how everything works.

If you haven't tried cooking before and you think it sounds tricky, you could get some practice in by microwaving soup or baking potatoes before you start, but the main thing is...

ENJOY YOURSELF!

GOD

PS: Words <u>like this</u> are explained more at the back of the book.

STEP ONE

GETTING PREPARED

All recipes work best with good preparation but making a cosmos requires more thought than most. To get it to work the way you want, it helps to have a plan that covers everything before you start...

GOD'S UNIVERSE PLAN:
(SHOPPING LIST)

WHAT DO YOU WANT TO MAKE

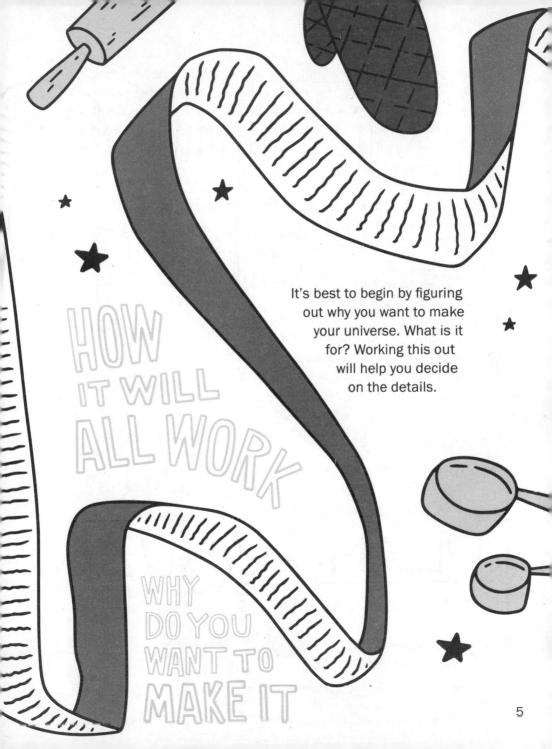

HOW IT WILL ALL WORK

WHY DO YOU WANT TO MAKE IT

It's best to begin by figuring out why you want to make your universe. What is it for? Working this out will help you decide on the details.

When you are planning a complete cosmos there are two friends of mine who will help. They were with me when I made this universe (the one you live in) so they know from experience how tricky it is to get everything to work. You might think they're hard to please, but they are wise and know a lot of the stuff you're going to need! Let me introduce you...

This demanding lady is her Right Royal Prima Dona-ness

QUEEN MARTHA MATIX

MY DEAR–
I simply wouldn't leave the house without the perfect equation for the occasion!

And her friend, <u>Maestro</u>

SIR PAYNIN THEOBAUM

FiRST LORD O͟F FFYSiCS

– Theo to his friends.

> You're 99.99999999999999 per cent right... but that's still 0.00000000000000001 per cent wrong – your universe will never work if you make HUGE mistakes like this!

He's extremely particular!

INGREDIENTS:

TO GET:

- ☐ Nothing
- ☐ NADA
- ☐ nichts
- ☐ ZILCH
- ☐ Rien du Tous
- ☐ COMPLETE ZIP

One of the good things about universe-making is that you don't have to do much shopping: the ingredients list is very short. To make one filled with stars, planets, <u>gravity</u>, trees and badgers, you need to start with pretty much nothing – no stars, no planets, no gravity, no trees, and absolutely no badgers!

The kind of high-quality 'nothing' you need for making cosmoses is **VERY** hard to get hold of in this universe and even harder to understand. I'm leaving what it looks like to your imagination...

ALL ABOUT 'NOTHING'

Most of us think 'nothing' is where there isn't anything. Pretty simple, right? But some scientists aren't so sure...

They're exploring all kinds of clever ideas about what sort of 'nothing' there might have been when our universe didn't exist. It is tricky to work this out because, whatever it was, it doesn't seem to exist anymore.

SO, WHAT KIND OF 'NOTHING' CAN WE FIND IN OUR UNIVERSE NOW?

What if we went looking around the deepest, darkest parts of space? Even there, scientists think we'd find roughly one tiny-weeny particle of stuff (one <u>atom</u>) in every cubic metre. That's like one atom in a fridge-sized chunk of space. This may not sound like much, but it's still something and there's also energy and radiation all over the place. Even gravity is a 'something' – and that's everywhere!

To cut a long story short, in this cosmos, 'nothing' is nowhere; it doesn't exist. You could say, 'nothing isn't' – which is kind of mind-blowing.

SETTINGS:

Most recipes will say something like: 'To make a good cake, set the oven to 200°C and put the mixture on the middle shelf for 30 minutes.' Making a universe is similar – only there are loads more settings to think about and trillions of trillions of trillions of <u>gazillions</u> of ways of making one that doesn't work at all or can't ever do what you want. It also takes a lot longer to cook.

Theo and Martha will make sure everything you make works the way you want, but they will insist you are extremely careful and precise about all the settings you choose.

We would just like to run through a few million important points...

We'll start with how hot you want the Big Bang, then how big you want your <u>electrons</u>...?

So, what kind of 'important points' are Theo and Martha talking about? What kind of details do you need to include in your universe plan?

First of all, you've got to choose exactly the right strength for the fundamental forces of nature you want to use.

GRAVITY

is a good example. If you make your gravitational force too strong your universe will crunch back together before it really gets going. On the other hand, if it's too weak the whole thing will spread out like a thin mist without making stars or anything else.

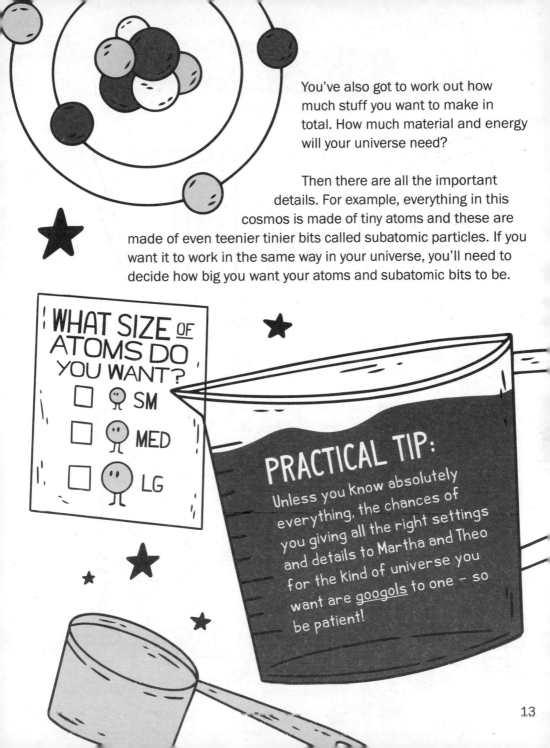

You've also got to work out how much stuff you want to make in total. How much material and energy will your universe need?

Then there are all the important details. For example, everything in this cosmos is made of tiny atoms and these are made of even teenier tinier bits called subatomic particles. If you want it to work in the same way in your universe, you'll need to decide how big you want your atoms and subatomic bits to be.

WHAT SIZE OF ATOMS DO YOU WANT?

☐ 😊 SM

☐ 🙂 MED

☐ 🙂 LG

PRACTICAL TIP:

Unless you know absolutely everything, the chances of you giving all the right settings and details to Martha and Theo for the kind of universe you want are googols to one – so be patient!

ATOMS AND 'SUBATOMIC' PARTICLES?

Most of the stuff we see in this universe is made of atoms. What makes one type of 'stuff' different from another is the kind of atoms it is made of. And what makes one kind of atom different from another is its own special number and combination of subatomic particles.

Every atom has an incredibly tiny centre called a nucleus made up of protons (positively charged bits) and neutrons (very dense bits with no charge).

This nucleus is surrounded by even tinier particles called electrons (negatively charged bits that weigh hardly anything) whizzing around. One hundred years or so ago, we'd already discovered about

90 DIFFERENT TYPES OF ATOMS

but we thought they were all made of just these three kinds of subatomic particles (protons, neutrons and electrons). Things have come a long way since then and we now know there are many different types of subatomic particles and they fall into two groups...

HAS ANYONE SEEN MY QUARK?

The first group are 'matter particles' – this includes protons, neutrons and electrons as well as funny things called quarks. Protons and neutrons are made up of quarks, and it's the quarks that give protons their positive charge. Scientists have also found 'anti-matter' particles which have opposite charges. If an electron comes into contact with an anti-electron (called a positron)...

KABOOM THEY DESTROY EACH OTHER COMPLETELY!

The second group are 'force particles' or 'bosons'. They carry energy, like light energy. The Higgs boson is very famous because scientists first predicted its existence in 1964. When they finally found it, after 40 years of looking, they were **VERY** excited because it showed their ideas had been right.

NUMBER OF ATOMS IN THE UNIVERSE

There are thought to be around 10^{80} atoms in the known universe – that's 1 with 80 zeros after it, which would look like this: 100 000 000 000 000 000 000 000 000 000 000 000 000 000 000 000 000 000 000 000 000 000 000 000 000 000

STEP TWO

THE BIG BANG

Once you've got your plan ready, you can move on to make time, space and everything in what's called a 'Big Bang'. Compared to getting all the details of your universe plan sorted out with Martha and Theo, it's a complete doddle – though it still involves some pretty tricky science. Even the best scientists on Earth are only just starting to understand the Big Bang that started this universe.

The key thing is to make sure your plan is exactly right. When you're happy with it, you're ready to make everything out of your 'nothing' and it should all arrive almost instantly. This is why it's called a 'Big Bang'. (By the way, it helps to be all-powerful for this bit.)

NOTHING

EVERYTHING

PRACTICAL TIP:
Stand well back and shield your eyes before your Big Bang happens or you'll be toast.

Just a word of caution because some of you might get a bit
disheartened at this stage...

Despite the name,

BIG BANGS CAN BE A BIT OF A LET-DOWN.

They might be fantastically hot and bright, and they might end
up with gazillions of stars, but they actually start out too small
for anyone to see.

The other disappointment is that they don't bang. You won't hear a thing – at least from the outside – because sound doesn't travel where the universe isn't.

IF YOUR BIG BANG, STARTS OFF INFINITELY TINY AND DOESN'T BANG – GOOD JOB!

WHO FIRST DISCOVERED THE BIG BANG?

In the early twentieth century, lots of physicists thought that the cosmos had always existed and hadn't ever changed much. But new work from several brilliant people changed this idea forever!

HENRIETTA LEAVITT

A young astronomer, called Henrietta Leavitt, helped to find a way to measure the huge distances between <u>galaxies</u> for the first time.

GEORGES LEMAÎTRE

Georges Lemaître (a physicist and a priest) was a genius at maths and his calculations all seemed to suggest the universe was expanding.

He also worked out that an expanding universe probably meant it started out incredibly small when time and space first started to exist. (This idea is what we now call the 'Big Bang'.)

EDWIN HUBBLE

An astronomer, called Edwin Hubble also found that the way the galaxies were actually moving meant that the universe really was expanding, just as Lemaître had predicted!

SIR FRED HOYLE

Although he wasn't a fan of the theory, British astronomer Sir Fred Hoyle came up with the name 'Big Bang'. He was actually making fun of the idea at the time, but the name stuck!

STEP THREE

EXPANDING YOUR UNIVERSE

The good news is you won't be disappointed for long... if you've got all the settings right, you'll notice your baby universe starts to inflate like a massive balloon almost as soon as your Big Bang has banged (quietly!).

PRACTICAL TIP:

Watch this closely. Cosmic inflation is incredibly fast, but it must slow down at exactly the right time or your universe is doomed. After this stage, you'll need to keep your universe expanding, but much more slowly.

If you want to create a universe like this one (the one you live in) and you've given Martha and Theo all the right settings to do that, the inflation phase will stop when your cosmos is only a tiny fraction of a second old. Be very careful at this point, because everything in your baby universe will still be unbelievably hot and bright. The important thing is to make sure you've got exactly the

RIGHT AMOUNT OF SPACE BETWEEN ALL THE STUFF

and exactly the right amount of stuff between all the space.

IF THERE'S TOO MUCH SPACE NOTHING INTERESTING CAN HAPPEN LATER,

but if there's not enough space and too much stuff, your universe will crunch together and collapse under its own gravity before it can properly get going. And you haven't got much wriggle room on this – one second after the Big Bang the ratio of stuff to space (the amount of material and energy compared to the amount of space) must be exactly right. You can check just how exact you need to be with Queen Martha Matix and the First Lord of Ffysics.

GOOD LUCK!

31

If your head is still spinning from a new universe bursting into existence and inflating ginormously all within the blink of an eye –

DON'T WORRY.

For the next few hundred thousand years you can chill out, alongside your new universe, as it cools and expands steadily.

At the end of this stage your universe should look kind of 'the same-ish' throughout, almost uniform... but not quite. You need some **VERY** slightly clumpy parts – areas where there's a tiny bit more warm stuff and less cold space than the rest –

OR YOU WON'T GET ANY GALAXIES AND STARS.

But don't overdo it. Imagine swirling half a teaspoon of cream cheese into a whole bath-full of soft vanilla ice cream – that's the kind of slight variation you're after.

THE 'AFTERGLOW' OF THE BIG BANG:
COSMIC MICROWAVE BACKGROUND

When you think of microwaves, you probably think of kitchen machines, but microwave radiation is actually found all over the universe and it's a kind of light you can't see with your eyes. In the 1960s, space scientists found some special microwaves and they realised it was actually the oldest light in the universe!..

Straight after the Big Bang, the universe was too hot and dense for light to travel very far (think of it as looking very foggy). But after about 380,000 years, the universe had cooled down enough to become more transparent, so light could travel really far and fast. The light that started travelling then is still travelling now, and that's what we see as Cosmic Microwave Background or CMB for short!

Two Americans called Penzias and Wilson discovered the CMB by accident. They were trying to use a sensitive detector to measure really faint signals, but whatever they tried, something kept interfering and it was 100 times bigger than anything they'd expected. At first they blamed a pair of pigeons who were nesting in their detector, but even after they'd moved the pigeons and cleaned up their poo, it didn't go away. They then realised that the interference wasn't coming from anything on Earth or even in our galaxy – it was

CMB!

Because light was able to start travelling long distances at about the same time all over the universe, the CMB is spread almost evenly across the cosmos. Scientists had predicted the universe would behave like this after the Big Bang, so it was great to find the evidence. What's also really cool is that the CMB shows us what the universe was like back at that very early stage, so we can see how things came to be as they are today.

Scientists got a clearer picture of the CMB by sending a special telescope into space which could detect microwave radiation. The picture sent back is one of the most important in science! It showed us that 380,000 years after the Big Bang our universe was nearly the same all over, but that some parts had just a little bit more stuff in than the rest. These are what grew into all the stars and planets and galaxies we see today!

IT WASN'T MY FAULT I TELL YOU!

STEP FOUR

MAKING STUFF

If you're making a universe that works like this one, it should be cool enough to allow light to travel and for atoms to form about 380,000 years after the Big Bang. Gravity can then start clustering the atoms together into clouds of gas. As these clouds get bigger and denser (thicker) they start attracting more and more gas and other smaller gas clouds – growing faster and faster. In the end some of the gas clouds get so thick and so huge they start to collapse in on themselves.

This should make them spin really fast, stirring up your cosmos nicely.

As the gas clouds collapse and spin they will get really, **REALLY** hot and, suddenly... woah –

YOUR KITCHEN
LIGHTS UP BIG TIME!

Do not panic; you haven't set fire to your tea towels! The light is from the first stars. This should start to happen about 150 million years after your Big Bang or about 149.6 million years after you got your first atoms. Trust me – it's worth the wait!

'SO WHAT EXACTLY JUST HAPPENED?'

I hear you ask...

...When the spinning gas clouds get big enough and hot enough, the little, tiny gas atoms start joining or 'fusing' together in a process called nuclear fusion. This makes new and bigger atoms of a different gas and releases a **HUGE AMOUNT** of energy in the process.

It's the release of all the energy from nuclear fusion that explains why stars are hot and bright and light up the sky.

NUCLEAR FUSION

Different types of atom each have their own specific number of protons in the nucleus and this makes them behave and interact in particular ways. We call each type of atom a different kind of

'ELEMENT'.

You've probably heard of some elements like hydrogen, oxygen, sulphur or carbon, but how are they all made?

Lots of it happens in stars, through a process called 'nuclear fusion'.

Nuclear fusion happens when two fast-moving atomic <u>nuclei</u> get close enough to fuse together making a new, bigger atom – a different element completely. When this happens, it produces unbelievable amounts of energy – it's what powers our sun and all the stars.

HOW NUCLEAR FUSION HAPPENS:

DEUTERIUM

HELIUM

Fancy forms
of hydrogen

TRITIUM

FUSION

ENERGY

NEUTRON

The sun and all similar stars in this universe are mainly made of atoms of hydrogen (the lightest of all the elements). At its centre the sun has temperatures of nearly 16 million degrees Celsius and pressures that are 250 billion times higher than they are on the Earth's surface.

It would not be a great place for people (!), but these are perfect conditions for fusing hydrogen into helium and warming up the solar system.

Many scientists are trying to get nuclear fusion to work as a source of clean energy for people to use on Earth. It's very difficult to get fusion reactors to high enough temperatures here on Earth, but if scientists can do it, they could power the world without coal, oil or gas and help slow down climate change. (See **In This Universe** box on page 154.)

STEP FIVE

ABOUT STARS

Stars are very important for a good cosmos. They are like fiery ovens making many of the interesting materials you are going to need for rocks and life.

It's very important you get the right balance of star sizes: some massive ones which explode violently and quickly and some small-to-medium ones, like your sun, which burn steadily for a very long time.

SO, WHAT EXACTLY DO STARS DO?

Well that rather depends how big they are...

PRACTICAL TIP:
Getting the right balance of star sizes in your universe early on is not just very important, it's also very tricky. Choose the right temperature and time settings for your Big Bang and you'll be OK, but just a featherweight wrong in either direction and... disaster! (Theo and Martha can explain why if you ask but it takes two days and 60 blackboards for them to explain – so only ask if you really want to know.)

Let's start with 'ordinary' small-to-medium-sized stars. They might not sound exciting, but it's being a bit boring that makes them so useful. You know precisely what they're going to do and they keep doing it for billions of years. In this universe, they hang around for <u>eons</u> fusing hydrogen into helium and more hydrogen into more helium and even more hydrogen into even more helium (you get the picture!), giving a nice steady amount of light and heat.

At the very end of their lives, they run out of hydrogen and start fusing helium into bigger atoms (like carbon and oxygen). This final stage of an ordinary star's life is often really interesting because they swell up until they become **HUGE**, bloated 'red giants'! (This is the real name and they really are red!)

I'M GOING TO BE A RED GIANT WHEN I GROW UP!

I'M NOT BORING!

Just to give you an idea how long small-medium stars usually last: your sun is about 4.5 billion years old now. At the end of its life, as it swells into a red giant, it will swallow up the planet Mercury, then Venus will disappear and it will be touch-and-go for Earth... it might get swallowed by the giant old sun or it might not. Really exciting – BUT you don't need to worry! None of this will happen for another 5 billion years.

MASSIVE STARS ARE EXCITING!

When they are born, they are up to 50 times more massive (heavier) than the Earth's sun and much more powerful.

If you were making soup instead of a universe, the massive stars would be like adding hot chillies. You need them to spice things up a bit, but if you have too many, nobody will be able to eat it!

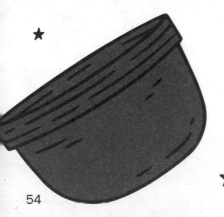

STAR SIZE GUIDES:

☐ **REGULAR STARS**
LIKE OUR SUN (about 1-2 million km across)

◻ **MASSIVE STARS** (about 3-5 million km across)

■ **RED GIANTS** – Regular stars near the end
of their life (about 1-2 billion km across)

Massive stars generate mega amounts of energy from the start, so they use up all their lightest elements a hundred or even a thousand times more quickly than ordinary stars. They also have enough power to start the next steps of fusion at an earlier stage and to make much bigger atoms.

This is very useful in any new cosmos because these huge stars are like factories for making many of the different elements that you are going to need later.

The big stars you can see from Earth make carbon and oxygen after helium (like ordinary stars do), but then the fusion process continues all the way to iron. If your universe works the same way, you should end up with your massive stars making 26 or so different elements, each of them with different sized atoms. And the whole process is turbo-charged! Massive stars only take a few million years to make all these elements, not the billions of years we talked about for ordinary stars...

SOME OF THE NEW ELEMENTS ARE GASES BUT MANY ARE METALS AND OTHER TOUGH STUFF.

Perhaps the best thing about massive stars comes right at the end of their lives when they've run out of fuel. By then they've grown into humungous monsters, thousands and millions of times bigger than the sun.

They get bigger and bigger then, all of a sudden, they

EXPLODE

... and the explosion is ENORMOUS.
It is called a supernova and it's like the best firework you've ever seen, only a million billion trillion times brighter and with enough energy to fuse together elements with even bigger atoms than iron.

HELLO??

Depending on exactly how enormous the star was, the supernova might explode everything out into space or – stranger than that – sometimes they leave behind a tiny but incredibly dense core, only about 10 km across but heavier than the sun. This is called a

NEUTRON STAR.

In this universe many neutron stars don't look like much because they are dark and tiny, but others rotate and shoot out beams of radiation. These are called pulsars. If that radiation beam points at the Earth on the way round, then scientists see a pulse of light through their telescopes every time it rotates. When the astronomers on Earth, like Jocelyn Bell Burnell, first spotted them, the pulses of light were so regular, they thought they'd found aliens signalling to them!

61

The biggest of all supernovae can leave behind something even more wonderfully weird: an ultra-dense object called a black hole.

You can think of a black hole as being a bit like a plughole in space – sucking everything in as it spirals in on itself. Once you're in the clutches of a black hole you get squashed and stretched so much that you are basically spaghetti! The scientific term for this is

SPAGHETTIFICATION!

(I kid you not!) Black holes are so dense that even light can't escape and they feed on anything that falls into them, including each other, till they grow supermassive.

Over time, you should start to see your stars, gases and black holes organise themselves into swirling clumps drawn and held together by gravity, usually, with a supermassive black hole in the middle. These are galaxies (like the Milky Way you live in). You'll probably see the first ones appear in your universe about a billion years after your Big Bang. Galaxies are enormous; each one might have hundreds of billions of stars, and they are useful in cosmos-cooking because they bring things closer together, which speeds up star formation.

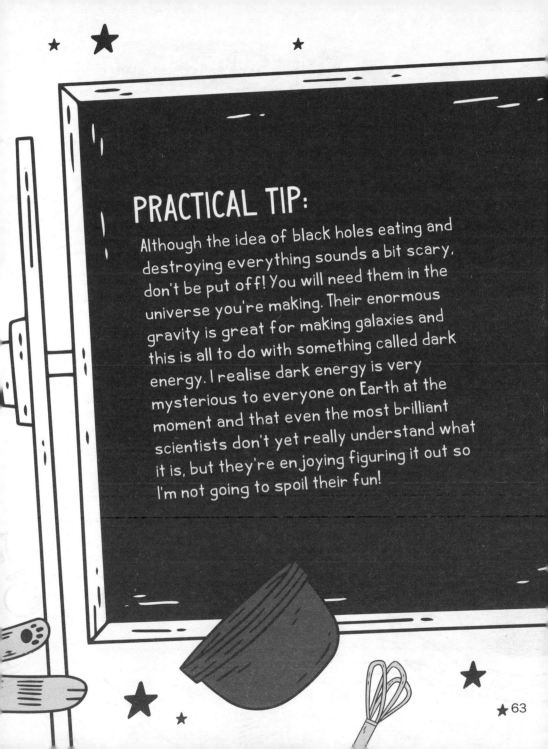

PRACTICAL TIP:

Although the idea of black holes eating and destroying everything sounds a bit scary, don't be put off! You will need them in the universe you're making. Their enormous gravity is great for making galaxies and this is all to do with something called dark energy. I realise dark energy is very mysterious to everyone on Earth at the moment and that even the most brilliant scientists don't yet really understand what it is, but they're enjoying figuring it out so I'm not going to spoil their fun!

BLACK HOLES

Black holes lurk around inside galaxies like invisible pits of doom eating anything that falls within reach of their **HUGE** and deadly gravitational pull. Most black holes are tiny – only about 16 km across – but still around 20 times the mass of our sun. Supermassive and ultramassive black holes are nearly always found in the centre of galaxies and are **MUCH** bigger – scientists now think they can be up to 40 billion times more massive than the sun and as big as our whole solar system.

Like a fly caught in a spider's web, any planet or star that gets too close to a black hole is trapped with no escape. It orbits around, spinning closer and closer until the black hole literally tears it apart, pulling the surface away and eating it bit by bit till there's nothing left. Amazing.

If two supermassive black holes get too close, they start spiralling in towards each other getting faster and faster – trapped in a dance to the death! When they merge it releases more energy than anything else in the universe – 100 million times more than a supernova (which is mind boggling!).

But black holes don't just destroy things. For example, the ultra-mega-ginormous energy of the biggest of these collisions is what creates some of the biggest atoms.

IT WOULD ALSO BE HARD FOR GALAXIES TO EXIST WITHOUT BLACK HOLES TO HOLD THEM TOGETHER.

When you're making universes, it's only the 'hugest' amounts of energy that can fuse the biggest atoms to make the heaviest natural elements you want. You might use supernovae explosions for example. Or would you prefer colliding two neutron stars together or getting two supermassive black holes to merge? It's these sorts of events that have enough 'oomph' to do the trick and you can use a mix of all three if you like.

STEP SIX

STARDUST AND PLANETS

Stars themselves and the incredible things that some of them become (like black holes, neutron stars and supernovae) are all amazing, but they're not just there to be fabulous. Between them, they make all the elements your universe is going to need and from these elements you can make pretty much everything else – including planets!

This is mind-blowing. It means everything you see around you, all the elements (atoms) in this whole universe are, honestly, stardust. How cool is that!

The enormous space explosions and collisions we've talked about are also useful for spreading the stardust around. The massive energy they release shoots the stardust for gazillions of miles, spreading it all over the universe. If you want a cosmos with planets around some of your stars and life on some of your planets, you're going to need to do the same thing –

MESSY BUT NECESSARY!

ELEMENTS AND THE PERIODIC TABLE

There are lots of different atoms and elements. An atom of the element hydrogen (H) has only one proton in its nucleus, helium (He) has two, lithium (Li) has three and so on, right up to iodine (I) with 53, gold (Au) with 79 and uranium (U) with 92 protons in its nucleus. As well as these naturally occurring elements, there are also synthetic (manmade) ones like oganesson (Og) with 118 protons, but they are generally very unstable and disappear almost as soon as they are made! The different numbers of protons and other subatomic particles in each atom

MAKE THEM BEHAVE AND REACT DIFFERENTLY

both to each other and to things like temperature.

In 1869 a scientist called **DMITRI MENDELEEV**

invented a way of organising all the known elements into groups. He saw that most were solid at room temperature with a few gases and two liquids – mercury (Hg) and bromine (Br). He then did experiments to see how they behaved and he arranged them, according to the results, into what he called the

'PERIODIC TABLE'.

Mendeleev was a smart cookie and as he arranged the elements into groups he found some spaces where none of the elements he had tested seemed to fit. He realised that some elements might not have been discovered yet –

SO HE LEFT THEM AS GAPS.

Over the following years more and more elements were discovered and all the gaps got filled in. The complete periodic table, with Mendeleev's grouping, is still used today.

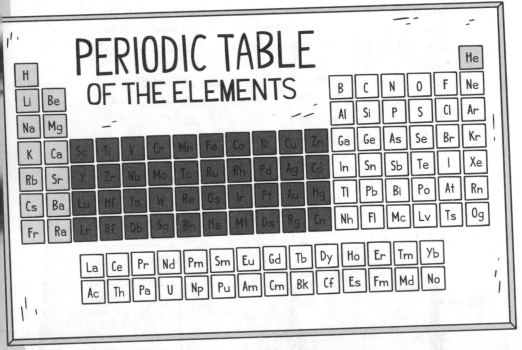

PERIODIC TABLE
OF THE ELEMENTS

H																	He
Li	Be											B	C	N	O	F	Ne
Na	Mg											Al	Si	P	S	Cl	Ar
K	Ca	Sc	Ti	V	Cr	Mn	Fe	Co	Ni	Cu	Zn	Ga	Ge	As	Se	Br	Kr
Rb	Sr	Y	Zr	Nb	Mo	Tc	Ru	Rh	Pd	Ag	Cd	In	Sn	Sb	Te	I	Xe
Cs	Ba	Lu	Hf	Ta	W	Re	Os	Ir	Pt	Au	Hg	Tl	Pb	Bi	Po	At	Rn
Fr	Ra	Lr	Rf	Db	Sg	Bh	Hs	Mt	Ds	Rg	Cn	Nh	Fl	Mc	Lv	Ts	Og

La	Ce	Pr	Nd	Pm	Sm	Eu	Gd	Tb	Dy	Ho	Er	Tm	Yb
Ac	Th	Pa	U	Np	Pu	Am	Cm	Bk	Cf	Es	Fm	Md	No

ISOTOPES

Atoms of a given element always have the same number of electrons and protons, but the numbers of neutrons in the atomic nucleus can sometimes vary. Hydrogen, for example, with one proton, usually has no neutrons, but you can find it with one neutron (deuterium) or even two neutrons (tritium) in its nucleus. These are all called isotopes of hydrogen. Carbon is similar. It normally has six protons and six neutrons in its nucleus (Carbon 12) but it can also be found as Carbon 13 or 14 isotopes with seven and eight neutrons respectively. Such rare isotopes are often useful and Carbon 14, for example, is used for 'carbon dating'.

At this stage, you might be thinking that getting the elements you need in your new cosmos sounds very straightforward. Stars fuse the smallest element to make the next smallest and then you get more fusing to make other larger elements like carbon and iron and then you get big space explosions and collisions with enough energy to allow elements with really big atoms to fuse together ... what could be easier – right?

I'M AFRAID NOT!

Making sure your universe has just the right amount of all the kinds of elements you need, particularly the ones that are important for getting life going, isn't just difficult, it's totally impossible unless you give Martha and Theo some very difficult and precise settings before your Big Bang. Scientists on Earth were amazed when they first discovered how tricky and unlikely it was for there to be the right amount of carbon and oxygen in this universe. (Details like this surprised scientists so much that some of them started to think I might have something to do with it!)

PRACTICAL TIP:

Don't hold your breath for your stars to make the right amount of carbon and oxygen or the equivalent life-important elements in your universe. It takes billions of years.

WHO MESSED WITH PHYSICS?

You might remember Sir Fred Hoyle from earlier (see page 25). He was the British astronomer and physicist who thought of the name 'Big Bang'. Fred was an absolute genius – a mega-brain – and most of his work wasn't about the Big Bang at all. He was mainly famous for figuring out exactly how the other elements were made from hydrogen and helium inside stars.

ABSOLUTE GENIUS

And it was while he was studying what stars did that he got stuck. He could see for himself that there is a lot of carbon around in this universe and he knew that all known life was based on it, but every calculation he did told him that it should have been all-but-impossible for stars to make any carbon at all, never mind lots of it.

THEN HE DID SOMETHING CLEVER

– he worked out that the only possible way a star could make carbon is by combining three helium nuclei together at once under very special conditions. But he knew that, for this to work, the nucleus of the carbon atom had to have some very peculiar and extremely unlikely properties. Before anyone had done any experiments he told his scientist friends exactly what weird and wonderful properties he thought the carbon nucleus must have, however unlikely it seemed. None of them believed it at first but, sure enough, when they did the experiments, they found he was exactly right. Years later, Sir Fred wrote this:

> '... A common sense interpretation of the facts suggests that a super-intellect has monkeyed with physics, as well as with chemistry and biology, and that there are no blind forces worth speaking about in nature. The numbers one calculates from the facts seem to me so overwhelming as to put this conclusion almost beyond question.'

It looks like Sir Fred's scientific discoveries led him to ponder ideas beyond the science, like the existence of a creator, although he never chose to believe in God.

PLANETS AND MOONS

Another great thing about stardust is that most of it doesn't stay dusty for long... it kind of tidies itself up!

Watch closely and you'll see that any ordinary star which starts life in the middle of a random cloud of mess quickly spins all the debris into distinct bands or disks of material as it rotates. Some of the bands might be gassy and others mainly dust and rock. They look a bit like bright halos orbiting around the star.

The halos look amazing in the star's light, but keep watching – it's about to get even more exciting! The debris in these halos can crash together to make larger and larger space objects. The bigger objects can then pull in even more and more debris! This process is called 'accretion'. When a halo band contains a lot of gas this process can make huge gas giant planets – like Jupiter and Saturn in the solar system where you live. And as long as the new star starts off with the right sort of big gassy bands, it all happens amazingly quickly... sometimes, within the first couple of million years of a star's life.

ACCRETION

also starts to happen in the halo bands that contain a lot of dust and rock bits, but in less of a rush. Over many millions of years you'll notice the biggest rocks in each band start to pull other smaller bits towards them, making clumps which turn into balls or spheres of material as they grow. It's great to watch, especially when you start to see the baby planets get hotter and hotter and denser and denser in the middle.

It's all a bit like making stars only on a much smaller scale so the temperatures and pressures never get high enough to cause nuclear fusion and burst into light (at least, not often!). Instead, the increasing heat and pressure melts everything inside the baby planet, making it fluid so all the heavier elements start to sink while the lighter ones float to the top, forming layers. Gradually a new planet appears, with a hard upper layer (the crust), a gloopy mantle of hot material underneath and a super-heated solid core made of something like iron and other heavy elements.

NOW, IF WE WERE MAKING CAKES

nobody would want the middle to be super-heated, but planets are very different and, as you'll see in the next step, molten middles are just what you want.

A decent-sized planet like your Earth doesn't cool down like a cake either... it can stay hot and fluid in the middle for a surprisingly long time: billions of years.

PERFECT!!

MOONS

are worth a separate mention – they too come in handy in the next step.

You should see a lot of moons being made by accretion in pretty much the same way as planets, but the rocks and bits of debris used this time are orbiting a planet, not a star. Moon formation can also happen in other exciting ways! For example, if two new planets orbiting the same star get too close! – guess what happens? It only takes a smallish meteorite strike to knock one planet into the other and...

KABOOM

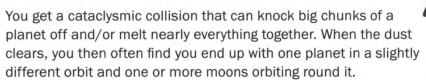

You get a cataclysmic collision that can knock big chunks of a planet off and/or melt nearly everything together. When the dust clears, you then often find you end up with one planet in a slightly different orbit and one or more moons orbiting round it.

Now things are really coming together: you've got gazillions of stars and things busy producing and distributing your elements, plus you've got solar systems under construction.

STEP SEVEN

FINDING THE RIGHT KIND OF PLANET FOR LIFE

If you're thinking of getting life going, allow about 9 – 10 billion years after your Big Bang. This is how long it's likely to take before the stardust floating round your universe should finally have enough of the elements you'll need in all the right places.

That said, you can't just jump in and get life started willy-nilly. If you want your cosmos to have living things, especially complex ones, there are still loads of other things you need to take care of first. One of the first things you need to do is to look around your universe and see which parts of it look promising – which bits look like they might be

GOOD 'NEIGHBOURHOODS' FOR LIFE?

PRACTICAL TIP:

Life does best with something solid to take root on – it's tricky to get it started just floating round in space like some sort of squidgy space slime!

You need to look for small- to medium-sized stars that would make good suns – living worlds need one that will burn brightly and steadily for billions of years, giving plenty of time for things to develop. You also want to be sure the solar systems you're looking at aren't still

'UNDER CONSTRUCTION'.

As you saw in step 6, the process of accretion involves a lot of crashing and melting together of rocks and stuff so life can't really get going till it tails off a bit.

Take a good look at the solar systems you've found that fit the bill.

THERE'S A LOT TO THINK ABOUT.

You're looking for planets that are just the right size and location in their solar system. The perfect planet for life has to be big enough to have its own <u>atmosphere</u> but not so big that high gravity will make that atmosphere thick and heavy or limit the sort of plants and creatures that can develop.

WHAT IF GRAVITY WAS DIFFERENT?

The Earth has stayed pretty much the same size since life began, so plants and animals – even single-celled organisms – have all evolved to live with gravity and work with it like it is now.

Earth's gravity can't change much... not unless the planet suddenly shrunk or grew, but it's funny to think what difference it might make to living things if it did...

I WANT TO EAT TREE LEAVES NOT GRASS!

If gravity suddenly increased for example, every creature that lived on land would feel much heavier. You might not be strong enough to walk uphill. Birds might not be able to fly. Giraffes wouldn't be able to hold their heads up and tall trees could fall over like skittles in a gust of wind. Most living things on Earth wouldn't be able to adapt very well at all.

Scientists have wondered about the sort of life that might evolve on planets with higher gravity. They think smaller and flatter plants and animals might do well – creatures like centipedes, for example, which are low to the ground and have a lot of legs to help them move around.

I'M GOOD!

WHAT ARE THESE FOR?

Another thing to consider is temperature. Check out the

ORBIT ★

of the planets you're looking at... you want ones that orbit their stars in a roughly circular pattern, just the right distance away so that most of their water (or your universe's water equivalent) stays liquid throughout the day and throughout the year. Any orbit which is too oval (elliptical) can lead to the surface freezing completely at some times of the year and getting boiling hot at others, which makes life difficult!

That's not to say you can't have a bit of snow (who doesn't love that?) and some hot, dry deserts, but if you want the kind of living things you see in this universe, they need liquid water, or your universe's equivalent, and a lot of it! They use it for all sorts of important internal processes including breathing properly, transporting food and oxygen, and keeping their temperature steady at the right level.

If it's anything like Earth, **ALL** the living things on your planet will probably need water or your equivalent. Life on Earth started in water and many plants and animals still live in it, including the world's biggest ever animal – the blue whale. I'm digressing now, but, at the other end of the scale, have you ever looked at a drop of pond water under a microscope? It's incredible. Like a mini-alien world teeming with

TINY PLANTS AND WIGGLY MICRO-MONSTERS.

WEIRD WATER

Have you noticed anything funny about water in the world around you? Usually, if you cool a liquid down till it starts to solidify, the solid bit is denser (heavier) than the liquid, so it sinks. This doesn't happen with water; when water starts to cool and freeze into solid ice, the ice is less dense than the cold liquid water around it, so it actually floats and that's important. It's another of those details you need to get exactly right when you're making your universe plan with Theo and Martha before you start. The properties and rules you choose – all those natural forces and particle sizes – must allow ice to float so that water can stay liquid in deep seas and lakes, protected by the ice layer on top. This helps living things keep safe in the liquid water underneath the ice so they can survive even the longest, coldest

ICE AGES.

MAKING ICE FLOAT

isn't always popular. It means you get icebergs – which are great for polar bears and seals, but they've also sunk a few ships over the years. On balance though, it would be much worse if a lot of water-based life died out every time you get a minor inconvenience like an <u>ice age</u>.

When you're looking for suitable planets where life might develop, you also need to remember they will be whizzing round stars, which are whizzing round in galaxies, which are themselves whizzing through space.

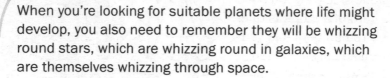

THIS IS A LOT OF WHIZZING <u>AND</u> SPACE IS A DANGEROUS PLACE!

You can think of that planet a bit like a spaceship of life – you've got to choose one with a good shield to protect it from being blasted.

A strong magnetic field usually does the job and will stop your creatures getting zapped. (I'm mainly talking about zapping by solar flares and deadly cosmic rays – not alien starships.)

Not every planet has a good magnetic shield so you need to be careful about this one. Do you remember I told you that, unlike cakes, molten middles were a good thing for planets? Well, this is where they come in... the super-hot molten metals in part of the core of the planet move around like hot syrup on a stove. The hottest material from the lower layers rises to the top, cools and drops back down again, creating a kind of circulation called a convection current. It's this that generates the electric currents that in turn create the magnetic field.

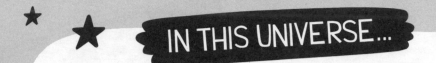

TECTONIC PLATES
VOLCANOES AND EARTHQUAKES

One of the side effects of a molten middle on Earth is that the rocky crust we all live on isn't as static and permanent as it looks. Volcanoes and earthquakes give us a clue about this.

The important molten outer core that gives the Earth its magnetic field is like a white-hot sea of molten metals about 6000 km below the planet's surface. Between this outer core and the hard rocks at the surface there is a thick layer of rock which is sort of goopy, and moves around slowly, because it's hot and being squashed under all the weight. The solid Earth's crust sits on top of this layer and is divided up into sections called 'tectonic plates' which are a bit like huge, slow-moving jigsaw pieces.

The tectonic plates move a few centimetres per year, carried by the convection currents in the hot goopy rock underneath. Over millions of years, this can move massive sections of land (including whole continents) huge distances: for example, in Earth's case, right from the Equator to the North pole!

Where one tectonic plate pushes on another, massive mountain ranges might be formed, like the Himalayas on Earth. Where they are pulling apart, molten rock seeps to the surface making a lot of volcanoes in one place and sometimes making new land. This is how Iceland was made – it grew out of volcanoes deep down in the ocean until it emerged from the sea 30 million years ago. There are lots of volcanoes in Iceland today and

THEY ARE STILL MAKING IT BIGGER.

Sometimes two neighbouring tectonic plates move or slide sideways, in opposite directions to each other, along what's called a 'fault'. Unsurprisingly, friction between the two plates means huge pressures build up along the fault over the years until, finally, the ground can't take it anymore and the plates slip, releasing all the pressure and moving the surface rock up to several metres all at once, in an earthquake. Some earthquakes are so big that nearby buildings and bridges are shaken to the ground and, if they happen in the sea, it can cause a tsunami.

CRUST

UPPER MANTLE

LOWER MANTLE

OUTER CORE

CORE

There are a million other things you need to think of, but I just want to give you one more example of how fussy you've got to be when searching out the right sorts of planets for life, and this one's also a lot of fun. Don't go thinking making universes is all work and no play...

YOU CAN GET REALLY CREATIVE WITH CREATION!

Moons are really useful when you are looking for where to get life started because they stop a planet from wobbling about too much – and nobody likes a wobbly planet. It's great watching them being made, but the really fun bit is in deciding how many moons you want and how far away you want them to be.

HOW MANY MOONS ARE TOO MANY?

I wanted a bit of variety in the solar system where you live. Jupiter has 79 moons of different sizes and Saturn has 82ish, but I opted for the elegant single-moon look for the Earth (Martha loved it!) and I also arranged everything so that, at least for a while, the moon looks pretty much the same size as the sun in the sky and can block out nearly all the sun's light. When this happens, it means the creatures living on Earth get to see a total

ECLIPSE...

A TOTAL ECLIPSE OF THE SUN

HOW AMAZING IS THAT?

We can't look at the sun directly because it would damage our eyes, but when scientists look at it through a special filter, they see that it looks about the same size in the sky as the full moon.

This is weird because the sun is actually 400 times bigger than the moon; it is 1.4 million km across while the moon is only 3475 km across. However, astoundingly, the sun is currently 400 times further away from Earth than the moon, which makes them look the same size in the sky.

It is even more amazing to realise that the moon has been very slowly moving away from Earth since it was formed. It's been much nearer for most of Earth's life and would have looked a lot bigger, but throughout human history the moon has been just the right distance away to match the size of the sun in the sky and give us a perfect solar eclipse. This means that, at the moment, if you are standing at the right place in the world when there is a total solar eclipse, the sun gets completely covered by the moon, making it dark. This really confuses all the birds and they start getting ready to roost. A total solar eclipse is also the only time we can see the super-hot gases surrounding the sun – its corona. Have a look at the picture on page 107... isn't that cool!

In a few million years the moon will have moved further away from the Earth making it too small in the sky to hide the sun completely, so an eclipse won't look nearly as good as it does now!

SUN

MOON

STEP EIGHT

LIFE BEGINS

Finally, once you've taken care of everything in Step 7, you should start to see life. You're going to love this part!

Just to give you an idea of timescales, in Earth's case, the planet formed about 9.5 billion years after the Big Bang and life got going about half a billion years after that.

It can be tricky to get life started and you are going to need two particular sorts of stardust. These (very) special elements are: **CARBON** and **OXYGEN**. If you're trying to make a universe with living things in it, you are going to need elements like these.

I'll tell you a bit more about oxygen later, but what makes carbon so useful is that lots of carbon atoms can join together into long chains or fancy shapes like hexagons. It can also combine with other elements like hydrogen, oxygen, nitrogen, phosphorous and sulphur.

All of this gives us some really, really useful new materials...

ATOMS AND MOLECULES

The atoms of some elements are always found on their own. It's not that no one likes them exactly, it's just that they are happy with the number of electrons they have so they don't feel any need to combine with anything else.

Helium's a bit like this. Unless a helium atom is in the middle of a star or massive space explosion, and being fused together with something else, you'll usually find it wandering about space on its own, comfortable with its own pair of electrons and with no particular plans.

As soon as an atom joins up with one or more other atoms, it's called a molecule. The atoms of some elements like to pair up with a best friend and become inseparable.

I'M GOOD!

Hydrogen, oxygen and nitrogen are all like this. You'll almost never find them on their own because they prefer to share electrons with one or two other atoms.

Some other elements, like carbon, are proverbial party animals! They love being in company and, as far as they are concerned, the more the merrier! You can end up with huge molecules containing 10s, 100s, 1000s or even more carbon atoms all linked together and a lot of other elements joining in.

Every atom in a molecule keeps its own protons and neutrons, but some of each atom's electrons start whizzing around the whole molecule in a mixed-up cloud. This is a bit like a creche of ducklings on a pond – nobody's ever certain whose ducklings are whose or where they all are exactly, but everybody's happy.

It's like that with the outer electrons in a molecule.

Under the right conditions you may eventually find some of the new mega-molecules made from your carbon-like 'party-animal' element have amazing potential to surprise you. Keep watching...

One or two of these molecules might start to do interesting things with energy absorbed from their sun and surroundings.

THEY MIGHT EVEN START MAKING COPIES OF THEMSELVES!

YOU LOOK FAMILIAR!

When you see this, it's time to get **MEGA-EXCITED** because using energy and making copies of themselves are two of the most important things living things can do and, to cut a long and complicated story short, these special new molecules can eventually clump together into teeny tiny slimy

LIVING GLOBULES. WOW!

GUYS, WHAT HAPPENED TO THE REST OF THE GANG?

Perhaps 'WOW' isn't what most people say when they see slime, but don't be fooled. It's amazingly wonderful and incredibly complicated inside. But even if you're not a fan, slimy living globules are only the start.

NOTHING STAYS THE SAME FOR EVER...

Living things change continually and in the end you should see a huge variety of life developing from those first living globules and spreading out all over the habitable bits of your planet – growing, crawling, squirming, swimming, flying and running! – all part of one

BIG, GIANT, HUGE FAMILY TREE!

(A bit like you and your Mum and Dad, and your grandparents and great grandparents only going back much, much, much further in time.)

Something you might have realised yourself by now is how important your original plan is, even for these later parts of cosmic cooking...

EVERYTHING

a universe needs to work – not just the stars and planets but details like making ice float, getting stars that last for a long time and making enough carbon and other elements from nuclear fusion – none of this is possible if you don't get all those settings right to start with. And that's especially true if you want life.

I'm guessing that going through the planning stage with Martha and Theo before you got cooking probably took ages, but you can see why they need to be so careful!

PRACTICAL TIP:
Don't ever call Martha or Theo 'fussy' – you'll never hear the last of it.

WHAT ARE LIVING THINGS MADE OF?

There are millions of different, weird and wonderful species alive on Earth today – from eagles and elephants to all kinds of gloopy algae. Despite this amazing variety, all living things we know of are made almost entirely of just six elements: carbon, hydrogen, oxygen, nitrogen, phosphorus and sulphur make up about 99 per cent of the weight of all the living stuff on this planet. Even more amazing is that 96 per cent of the weight is made up of just carbon, hydrogen, oxygen and nitrogen.

That's not to say other elements aren't important – for example, humans couldn't live without iron in our blood, calcium in our bones or iodine in our thyroid gland – but these other elements are only needed in small amounts.

DON'T FORGET THESE!

IRON

CALCIUM

At the moment, nobody knows if it's possible for alien or extraterrestrial life to be made of different stuff, but because all the living things on Earth need these six elements, scientists have decided that looking for them is a good place to start when they are looking for life on other planets.

OTHER CHEMICAL ELEMENTS (3.5%)

NITROGEN (3.5%)

HYDROGEN (9.5%)

CARBON (18.5%)

OXYGEN (65%)

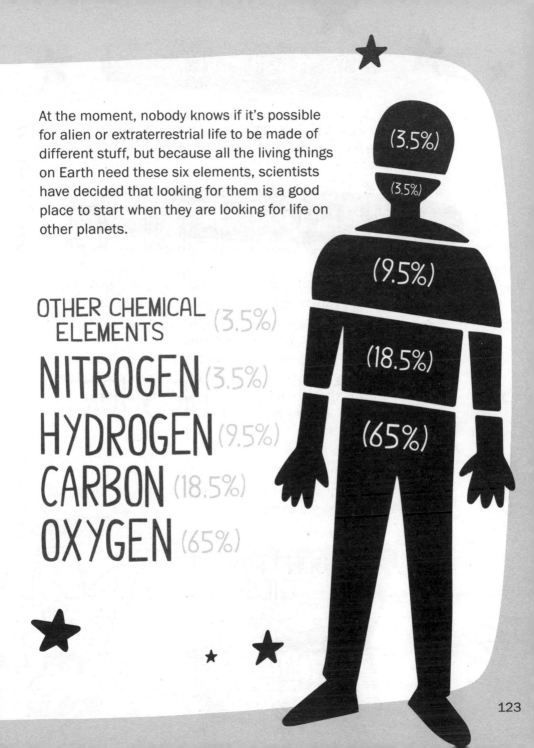

So how do we get from a planet covered in slimy living globules to the kind of world with loads of different living things in it?

THERE'S A LOT TO THIS—SO LISTEN UP!

All living things make copies of themselves. (It's one of the ways you can tell if something's alive... rocks aren't good at it.) On earth, almost all living things use the same carbon-based super-power molecule for the copying process. It's called deoxyribonucleic acid or

'DNA' FOR SHORT.

DNA IS FOUND

within the cells of living things (organisms) and combines a lot of carbon atoms with atoms of nitrogen, oxygen and hydrogen all arranged into special building blocks called 'bases' which link up, like beads in a necklace, to make a strand. Two of these strands then join together, base to base, in a beautiful spiral-shaped chain, a bit like a microscopically-tiny twisted ladder.

You're going to need the same or something very similar.

The order of the bases in the chain is really important: it's like a code or computer program that controls how each living thing grows and does things.

EVERY TYPE OF LIVING THING HAS ITS OWN UNIQUE DNA CODE

which it copies and passes to the next generation. It's what makes a banana palm a banana palm, an ant an ant and a human a human.

BANANA

ANT

126

Some living things, like the first slimy, living globules you might see on your planet, make copies of (or reproduce) themselves all on their own. Other living things that come later on might reproduce in pairs. But, however it happens on your planet, it will involve living things making copies of the DNA-type molecule which will be passed on to the

NEXT GENERATION.

HUMAN

Now, this next bit sounds weird, but roll with me... One of the cleverest parts in all this is how the

COPYING STEP CAN GO WONKY!...

Every time DNA is copied, there's a chance of little mistakes being made that change the code. It's one of the reasons why no two living things on earth are identical... Even the simplest living slime globule will have a pattern of DNA building blocks that's not exactly the same as its parent and won't be exactly the same as the next globule it makes either.

A lot of the time, the tiny differences in DNA code

DON'T REALLY CHANGE HOW THE ORGANISM WORKS.

but that's not always the case. Sometimes the mistakes stop
the new organism working properly and other times they help
it thrive better in its habitat than its parent did.

WHAT
HAPPENED?

SPOT THE DIFFERENCE!

The new slime globule in the picture has a tiny DNA difference that helps it absorb energy better than its parent. This

HELPS IT LIVE LONGER

and make more copies of itself than the original, so it can pass on its helpful DNA difference to lots of new copies. This might not sound like a big deal, but, over time and many generations, lots of these little differences can add up to really big changes in the way living things look or behave. This process is called evolution and it's so cool to see it in action!

DNA changes can help living things to evolve and adapt to a new habitat or different conditions where their ancestors wouldn't have **SURVIVED.**

On Earth, one of the most famous people for first working out that little changes might add up to big changes over time is

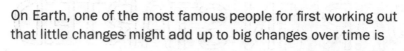

CHARLES DARWIN.

Way back in the 1800s, long before anyone on Earth knew about DNA, he was on a voyage of discovery all round the world and found himself on a tiny little island group called the Galapágos. They were miles and miles from anywhere else in the middle of the

HUGE PACIFIC OCEAN.

PACIFIC OCEAN

DARWIN STARTED TO NOTICE THE BIRDS...

A bird expert told him that they were all closely related types of finch, but they had different shaped beaks depending on the type of food they ate – soft fruit, hard seeds, insects...

A light started to dawn in Darwin's brain.

He started to think that all these different types of bird might

HAVE COME FROM JUST ONE SPECIES

of finch that had arrived on the islands long ago.

All the first generations of finches that came from these original arrivals would have looked pretty much the same, with very similar beak shapes to their parents. But as the population of finches grew and spread out across the islands, any tiny differences in beak shapes that that made a bird better at eating the kinds of food available in its area, helped that bird raise more young.

OVER TIME, THIS KIND OF BEAK SHAPE

would then become more and more common wherever that food was found.

As he kept studying the birds, Darwin realised how multiple generations of tiny changes would add up, and could explain why the finches in one place looked and behaved differently to those living in other parts of the Galapagos. Each type of finch had adapted to the particular food and environment where they lived.

Of course Darwin didn't know about DNA at the time, (scientists on Earth didn't work out what that was till the 1900s) but he'd have loved to know about this amazing molecule and the beautiful biological code which lets evolution work!

DON'T HOLD YOUR BREATH FOR EVOLUTION THOUGH:

like so many other parts of making a universe, life can't be rushed. First it'll probably take around 10 billion years from your Big Bang, till you've got enough of all the important elements where you need them. Then, after the 'WOW' moment of finally seeing your first slimy life forms,

NOTHING MUCH SEEMS TO HAPPEN FOR EONS.

Two and a half thousand million years after I saw the first tiny slimy living globules appear on Earth, living things had spread out all over the place and developed a few more fancy colours, but they were still, basically, glorious slime!!

If you're hoping to make things like daisies, dogs and piranhas, you've just got to be

PATIENT.

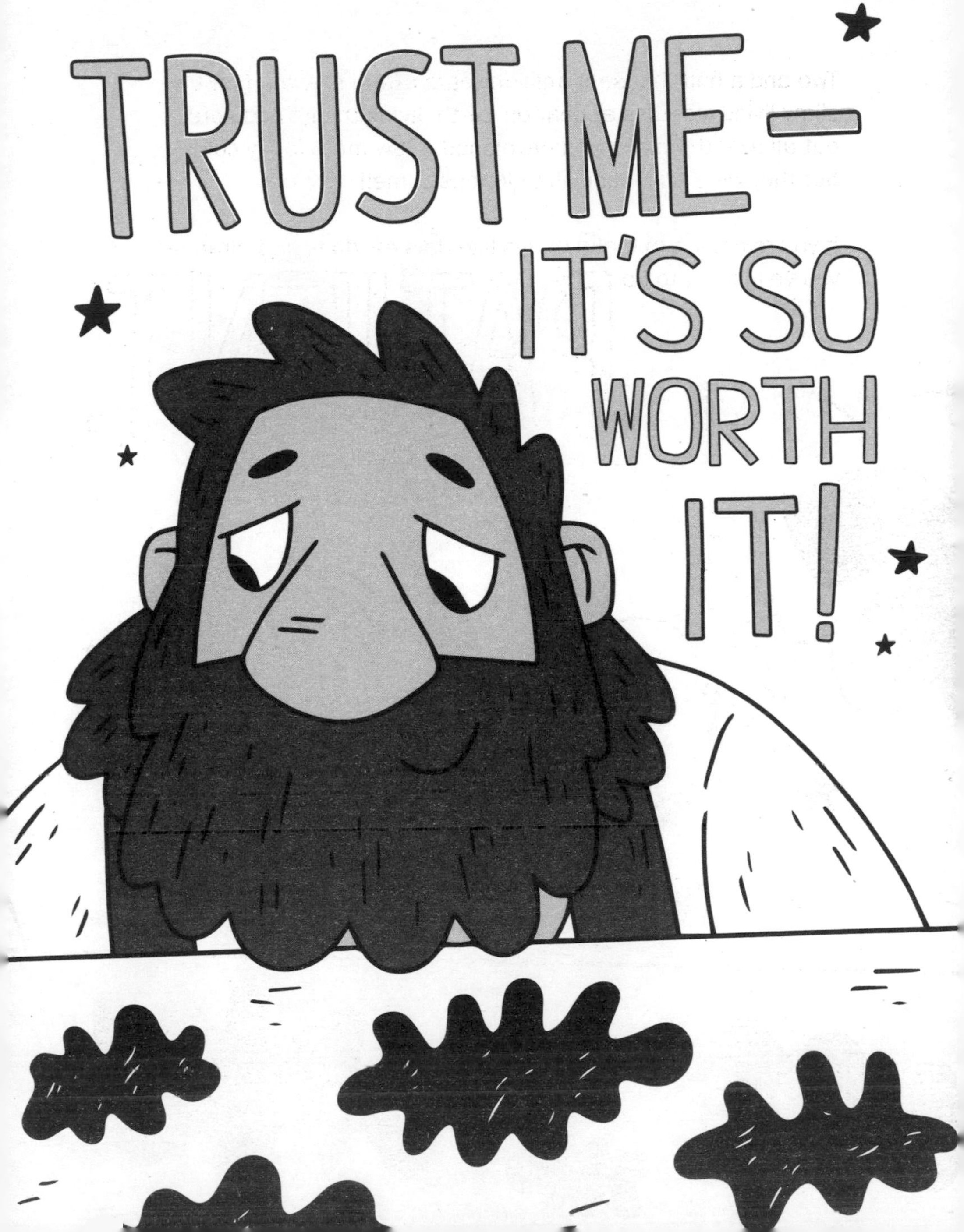
TRUST ME –
IT'S SO WORTH IT!

STEP NINE

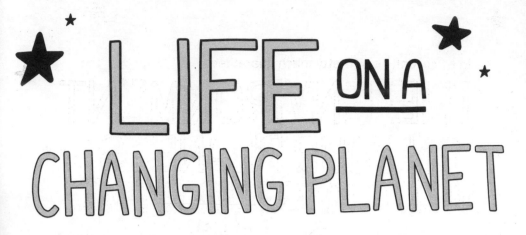

LIFE ON A CHANGING PLANET

Great job for getting this far and if you start to feel this next bit sounds a bit complicated, stick with it.

THE SCIENCE IS AMAZING...

I've been telling you about how life evolves gradually. Well, the other thing you've got to bear in mind is that your planet will always be changing too. Often this process happens slowly, but sometimes planetary changes can be fast and dramatic.

In any event, I can pretty much guarantee

THE ENVIRONMENT ON YOUR PLANETS WILL CHANGE OVER TIME.

The surface might get hotter for a while, for example, and then cool back down. Or the gases in the air (atmosphere) on your planet might change completely over time.

Obviously, this complicates things because you've got a lot of things changing at once, but the good news is that

EVOLUTION CAN HELP LIFE ADAPT.

Hooray for evolution when you think about it... if life couldn't evolve and adapt to a changing environment, everything could die out when something new or unusual happens on your planet which it definitely will, all the time!

WATCH OUT!

Now, most of the planetary changes you see will be slow, small and steady, but it's sometimes

FAST AND FURIOUS!

I'm talking about sudden environmental change and BIG natural events like earthquakes, tsunamis, catastrophic floods, meteorite strikes, supervolcanoes and the arrival of ice ages – just to mention a few!

Anything like this tends to leave devastation in its wake – it's a 'natural disaster' if you're an organism living in the affected zone. BUT, are things like these nothing but a catastrophe – clouds with no silver lining whatsoever?

That's a hard one. It's unarguably a disaster for any organism that gets splatted by a meteorite strike, BUT the more you think about the kind of events we're talking about, the more you realise they tend to be side-effects of other really useful processes that any universe needs.

METEORITES,

for example, are part of planet formation and you wouldn't get far without that. Volcanoes, tsunamis and earthquakes often happen because of the molten and goopy layers deep under a planet's surface, but, without this, you can't get the magnetic fields you need to shield planets and life from dangerous space radiation.

WHY DO
WE NEED
THESE
AGAIN?

So, while it's true that there can seem to be downsides to many of the things a planet needs for starting and protecting life, you can see we're not really talking about clouds with silver linings, more like

SILVER LININGS
WITH SOME CLOUDS.

Whatever you think about this, one thing's for sure: major environmental change and big natural events certainly mix things up. You'll find some types of living organisms won't be able to cope or adapt quickly enough to whatever's happened and life will get really hard for them but, at the same time, it will give others the big break they need.

All this happened to Earth, several times in its history...

66 MILLION YEARS AGO FOR EXAMPLE...

There were all sorts of spectacular creatures living happily on Earth at that time, from huge dinosaurs (like Triceratops and Tyrannosaurus Rex) and reptiles (like giant, flying Quetzalcoatlus) to little mammals and other creatures.

When suddenly, a massive meteorite, about 12 km across, hit the Yucatan Peninsula of Mexico and pretty much shook the whole world. The explosion was so huge that it left a crater 180 km across that you can still see today, and so much dust was blasted into the atmosphere that it blocked the sunlight and changed the climate for years.

MANY SPECIES DIDN'T MAKE IT,

including most of the dinosaurs, but those that survived the strike itself and the big changes that followed were then able to take advantage of the habitats and opportunities left behind by extinct species.

SO SORRY GUYS!

THE SURVIVORS

included crocodiles, lots of fish and insects, some tiny mammal-like creatures and a few avian dinosaurs – aka prehistoric birds. It's hard to picture, but, over millions of years, the descendants of these remaining dinosaurs have evolved into the birds fluttering around you today. If anyone asks you what happened to the dinosaurs – point at the nearest pigeon.

You'll have figured this out for yourself by now, but in this part of cosmic cooking it's often a case of

'TWO STEPS FORWARD <u>AND</u> ONE STEP BACK'.

Things like a major meteorite strike or dramatic climate change on your planet can seriously set life on your planet back for a while.

But be patient... over billions of years, through all the ups and downs, you'll see trillions of different species come and go – evolving, adapting and becoming more and more diverse or different over time.

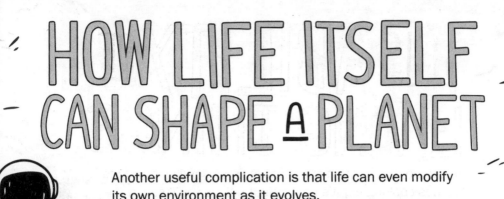

HOW LIFE ITSELF CAN SHAPE A PLANET

Another useful complication is that life can even modify its own environment as it evolves.

This is exactly what happened in the early days of life on Earth. Originally, the Earth's atmosphere was nothing like the air you breathe now: it had hardly any oxygen in it and so the earliest slimy living globules on Earth didn't need or use much oxygen. Instead, they started to make it! Over eons, more and more oxygen accumulated in Earth's atmosphere. This allowed living organisms to get more energy out of their food and made it much easier for complex life forms to develop. Nearly everything living on Earth today needs oxygen.

THIS ABILITY OF LIVING THINGS

to change their own environment is very useful when you're cosmos-cooking but it's not without risk as you'll see in the next **In This Universe** box... Just be careful if and when you get any intelligent creatures living in your universe. Do what you can to encourage them to act wisely and be careful how much you allow them to change things!

THREE BILLION YEARS AGO, YOU'D THINK EARTH WAS AN ALIEN PLANET AND YOU'D NEED A SPACE SUIT TO BREATHE.

MAN – MADE CLIMATE CHANGE

There's a bit of a problem on Earth at the moment because people are burning a lot of fossil fuels (coal, oil and gas) every day to generate energy. What's wrong with this, you might think? People need energy to do all sorts of important things, like keep warm, cook, travel and make everything from buildings to computers, so why is it bad?

The main problem is that burning fossil fuels, and other human activities, release greenhouse gases (like carbon dioxide CO_2). These

GREENHOUSE GASES

aren't bad in themselves: plants use CO_2 to make food, for example, and it acts like a blanket in the atmosphere, trapping heat energy like a greenhouse does, and keeping the world warmer than it would otherwise be. This is normally great because it stops the Earth becoming a 'snowball' planet, but currently we're burning fossil fuels so fast that CO_2 levels are getting too high and things are starting to go wrong. That nice warm blanket in the air around the Earth is now trapping too much heat. It's as if you had a lot of thick covers on your bed in the middle of summer –

YOU'D COOK!

It's having serious effects on the climate all around the world. Many places are getting hotter, and a few are getting colder or wetter because of changing weather patterns. More and more high temperature records are being broken each year and this is causing everything from

DROUGHTS AND WILDFIRES TO HUGE STORMS AND FLASH FLOODS.

Life is becoming a hard struggle for the families and animals living in some places, and many species will find it hard to adapt to such a large and fast change.

The good news is that we understand a lot more now about the science behind climate change, which means we know how to fix it! If humans stop burning so much fossil fuel, then natural processes, like plants and algae sucking up CO_2, would eventually help to bring the level of greenhouse gases in the atmosphere back down to a healthier level for life on Earth.

THE SITUATION IS URGENT,

but if we all work together, we can put it right.

Politicians, scientists and engineers are working on solutions. We've all seen solar panels and wind turbines that generate energy without burning fossil fuels. Other important research is looking at additional new technologies which might help: better ways of capturing greenhouse gases from factory chimneys; using hydrogen instead of petrol to fuel cars; and finding ways to speed up the removal of excess greenhouse gases that are already in the atmosphere.

WHAT ABOUT YOU?
CAN YOU DO ANYTHING?

Sure you can! Every time you switch off a light or find ways of using less energy in your house or school, you are making an important difference.

CREATIVE CREATURES

Along with your Big Bang, making stars and everything else, getting life going is definitely one of the best bits of cosmic cooking. And now, depending on what you put in your original plan and how patient you are, you might find that

14 BILLION YEARS OR SO AFTER YOUR BIG BANG,

some of your life forms evolve to the point that they are able to ask you questions and explore your creation for themselves. When and if you get something like this, it's another 'WOW' moment! You might think it's the best bit of all!

It's what happened on Earth when human beings like you came along, about 13.8 billion years after this universe got started –

WHAT A MASTERPIECE!

I love people – such clever, creative and inventive creatures. And so curious – always wondering about things and exploring everything they find. It's fantastic to see them figuring out how things work in this universe, and discovering all the settings and natural laws that Martha and Theo helped with.

IT'S TRUE

people can be selfish and have still got a lot of learning to do, but they can also be amazingly kind and loving. When and if you get similar intelligent creatures in your universe, they should reach the stage where they've learned enough to take care of each other and their planet.

They'll build hospitals, paint pictures, care for their environment and set up schools and universities to pass on knowledge and research new things.

I've given human beings a BIG responsibility in this universe. One of their jobs is to use and look after my creation carefully. We've got a lot in common. They are like my representatives, sharing my fascination with the cosmos and

I LOVE WATCHING HUMANS DISCOVER AND INVENT THINGS...

CAN YOU IMAGINE

the excitment of being the first scientist on Earth to understand how DNA works or to figure out the intricate beauty of it? Picture your own mind boggling as you suddenly realise the amazing variety of plants and animals and how they're all part of one massive family tree going back through the eons. (This might all sound obvious now I've told you about it, but 200 years ago no one on Earth would have ever guessed.) It's taken the work of thousands and thousands and thousands of scientists just to find out what's known on Earth today and they've got

SO MUCH MORE <u>TO</u> DISCOVER.

I want to give you one particular example of the scientific research people are doing on Earth – it's no more interesting than all the others, but this one is useful to know when you're making universes.

The study of life's history on Earth all started with people finding weird-looking rocky skeletons, and other mysterious shapes embedded within the layers of rocks on Earth. Lots of these looked a bit like parts of animals or plants, but very different to the living things people knew from the world around them. What were they, and where did they come from? It took a lot of thinking about but, in the end, people started to realise that they might be the traces of plants and creatures that

LIVED **ON** EARTH LONG AGO.

Nowadays, people know that these rocky remains (fossils) are essentially rock copies of long-ago living things, like plants and animals or sometimes their footprints or their poo! When they died, their bodies were buried in sand, mud, volcanic ash or other sediments and were ultimately trapped in the rocks and turned into rocks and minerals themselves as more and more mud and sediment piled on top of them. Then, over time, as their rocky surroundings shifted or got worn away by weathering, the fossils ended up back close to the surface of the ground again, ready to be found and puzzled over by humans.

In the end, geologists (the scientists who study rocks) were able to work out that different layers of rocks (and the fossils within these layers) were formed at different times over the history of Earth. That means that they've been able to use the fossil record to work out what types of creatures have lived on Earth and when. This was one of the keys that helped them realise that life on Earth had been changing over time, paving the way for Darwin's big discoveries!

If you put together a timeline from the parts of the fossil record they've worked out so far it'll give you a useful example of what you might expect from life on a planet in your universe...

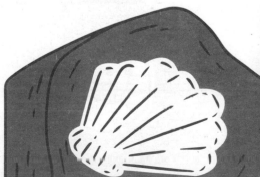

AN APPROXIMATE TIMELINE OF

★ MYA = Million of Years Ago

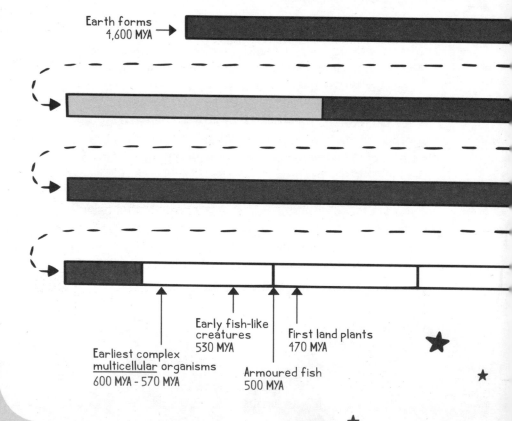

Earth forms
4,600 MYA →

Earliest complex <u>multicellular</u> organisms
600 MYA - 570 MYA

Early fish-like creatures
530 MYA

Armoured fish
500 MYA

First land plants
470 MYA

LIFE ON EARTH

★ All dates represent scientists' best current understanding, based on latest fossil record discoveries.

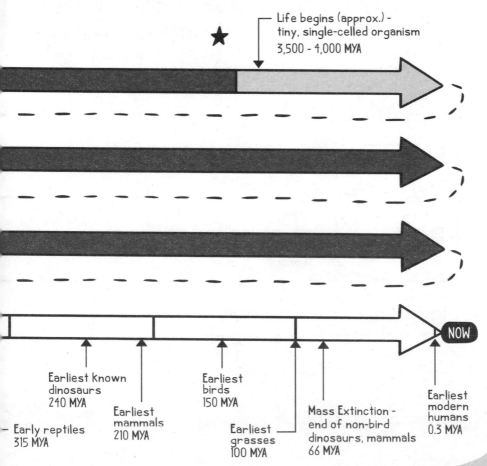

Life begins (approx.) - tiny, single-celled organism 3,500 - 4,000 MYA

NOW

Earliest known dinosaurs 240 MYA

Earliest birds 150 MYA

Early reptiles 315 MYA

Earliest mammals 210 MYA

Earliest grasses 100 MYA

Mass Extinction - end of non-bird dinosaurs, mammals 66 MYA

Earliest modern humans 0.3 MYA

Whatever the exact timeline of life's evolution on the planet you make, you can see it's likely to keep you very busy with

NEW SPECIES DEVELOPING AND CHANGING CONSTANTLY

– all the time you have life on your planet!

As time goes on, you'll be amazed by the creatures and plants that end up living in every nook and crevice of your world. If you get some human-like creatures who enjoy exploring, learning about and taking good care of your world,

IMAGINE THE FUN

they'll have piecing it all together!

STEP TEN

THE BIG PICTURE

Well, that's just about covered all the most important parts of a universe recipe. How did you get on?

Did you end up with the cosmic equivalent of a perfect sponge cake or did everything sink and stick to the pan? One of the best things about creating a cosmos is how you can enjoy ALL of it – every part of the making, and everything you make.

However, despite what a lot of people think, you can't just get a universe to a particular stage and then find something else to do. Oh no! It's not like that at all. It's pretty much a continuous process once you've started... and you'll be needed all the time.

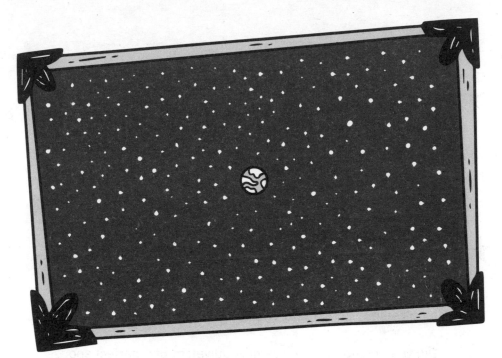

Think of the millions of billions of creatures living and depending on planet Earth, including your family, your friends and all the people and pets you love. Think of everything that matters a lot to you, and to them, and then think of all the people and creatures you don't know – to all the dolphins and pelicans and ants and fleas.

When you make a universe, every big thing and every little thing is relying on you; you can't take your eye (or your heart) off anything you've made, not even for a gazillionth of a second.

IT'S A FULL-TIME JOB.

And it's not just about making sure all the physical parts of your universe keep working well. You made your cosmos for a reason, remember, and you need to make sure these plans stay on track, especially if creatures like humans are in the mix.

There's truly nothing more wonderful in the whole recipe than getting intelligent beings that can talk to you, but they won't half complicate things! Exactly how I've taken care of all this on Earth is a huge and exciting story,

BUT THAT'S A TALE FOR ANOTHER DAY.

A BIT MORE INFORMATION ON SOME OF THE WORDS

ASTEROIDS

Asteroids are rocky objects, much smaller than a planet, that orbit a star like the sun.

ATMOSPHERE

The layer of gases all around a planet that allow living organisms to breathe.

ATOM

All stuff (matter) is made of atoms and they are tiny – only 0.1 to 0.5 nanometres or 0.1 to 0.5 billionths of a metre across. Atoms are so small that 12 grammes of carbon (about 2 teaspoonfuls) contains just over 6 x 10 x 10 x 10 x 10 x 10 x 10 x 10 x 10 x 10 x 10 x 10 x 10 x 10 x 10 x 10 x 10 x 10 x 10 x 10 x 10 x 10 x 10 x 10 (6×10^{23}) atoms of carbon. It takes the world's best electron microscopes to see atoms and it is amazing to think that they're made of even tinier bits. (See **In This Universe** box on subatomic particles on page 14.)

COMETS

Comets are smallish space travellers – a bit like asteroids, but made of frozen gases, rocks and dust and with weird elliptical (oval) orbits, which means that sometimes they are near their star (e.g. the sun) and sometimes they are far away. When they get near the star, they warm up, releasing some of the ice into a gas that can trail behind the comet like a bright tail.

ELECTRONS

Electrons are negatively charged subatomic particles which either whizz around inside an atom (attracted by the positive charge in the atomic nucleus) or join a cloud of other electrons whizzing around a molecule. (See **In This Universe** box on atoms and molecules on page 15.) Sometimes they wander off, attracted by another positive charge, and when gazillions of electrons move together, in the same direction, it becomes an electric current.

EONS

Often when people say 'eons' they just mean 'ages' or 'a very long time'. That's how we've used it in this book.

GALAXIES

Galaxies are collections of billions of solar systems plus extra stars, asteroids, dust and gas, all swirling around each other and held together by gravity. Many have a spiral shape (including our Milky Way), but there are also elliptical ones, and some that are just called 'Peculiar'! All galaxies are huge! The Milky Way, for example, is estimated to have 100 billion stars and it measures about 1,000,000,000,000,000,000 km across. Even light takes nearly 100,000 years to cross it.

GAZILLIONS

Not a real number (or even a real word until recently) but now recognised as a general term for unspecified large numbers. If someone told you they'd fallen off their bike gazillions of times, you'd probably say they were safer walking.

GOOGOL

An actual humungous number, namely 10^{100} or 1 with 100 zeros after it. To give you an idea how big it is, it is a LOT more than all the atoms in the whole universe.

GRAVITY

Gravity is the force of attraction between two objects. The more massive the objects and the nearer they are together – the bigger the attraction. It's the Earth's gravitational pull that holds the atmosphere and all of us on the surface of the planet. It stops anything, including us, drifting off into space. Only helium atoms are light enough to escape Earth's gravity and sneak off into space after a while – that's why it's not very common here on Earth.

ICE AGE

An ice age is when the surface temperature of the Earth gets about 6°C (or more) lower than it is now and it usually lasts for tens of thousands of years. When an ice age happens the ice sheets covering the North and South Poles grow to cover more and more land, trapping a lot of extra water and causing sea levels to drop.

MAESTRO

A master musician. Usually the conductor of a big orchestra or one of the best musical instrument players in the world.

METEORITES

Meteorites are rocky or metallic pieces of space debris, often parts of asteroids or comets, that travel from outer space to land on a planet like Earth. Most meteorites get burnt up in the planet's atmosphere on the way down, but some make it all the way through to the ground. If a big meteorite hits the Earth it can be very dangerous (ask the dinosaurs!).

MOONS

Moons are rocky satellites orbiting around a planet. So far, we've found over 200 of them in our solar system, varying in size from a castle to a small planet. Mercury and Venus are the only planets without any moon. Earth has one moon, Mars has two small ones and our largest neighbours – Jupiter and Saturn – have lots. Scientists have spotted eighty-two moons around Saturn and about seventy-nine around Jupiter. Some of Jupiter's moons are tiny, but fifty-three are big enough to have their own names.

MULTICELLULAR

To say a living organism is 'multicellular' just means it has more than one cell. Bigger, more complex, organisms like us have trillions of cells, including lots of different types, each doing different jobs.

NUCLEI

This is the plural of nucleus, talking about more than one nucleus.

Before I go, has anybody seen the cat?
Mr Schrodinger has lost him.

MISSING

CAT

AUTHOR'S NOTE:

I wouldn't have been able to write this book without the faithful encouragement of my friends in 'Christians in Science' (CiS) and extensive technical and editorial input from the team at The Faraday Institute for Science and Religion in Cambridge. I will always be grateful.

I also want to thank the publishing team at Hodder Faith for sharing my, CiS's and Faraday's enthusiasm for science and faith and for allowing this book to become a reality. It has been so good to work with Patrick Laurent and his illustrations have brought the ideas in this book to life in ways that have delighted me at every turn.

My final thank you is to God: for the constant encouragement and inspiration during preparation of this book, including the following Bible verses...

JOHN 1:3-5

Through him all things were made; without him nothing was made that has been made. In him was life, and that life was the light of all mankind. The light shines in the darkness, and the darkness has not overcome it.

PROVERBS 8:1a & 27, 30 - 31

Does not wisdom call out? ...

... I was there when he set the heavens in place, when he marked out the horizon on the face of the deep...

... Then I was constantly at his side. I was filled with delight day after day, rejoicing always in his presence, rejoicing in his whole world and delighting in the human race.

JOB 28:12b-13 and 38:33

Where does understanding dwell? No mortal comprehends its worth; it cannot be found in the land of the living.

Do you know the laws of the heavens?

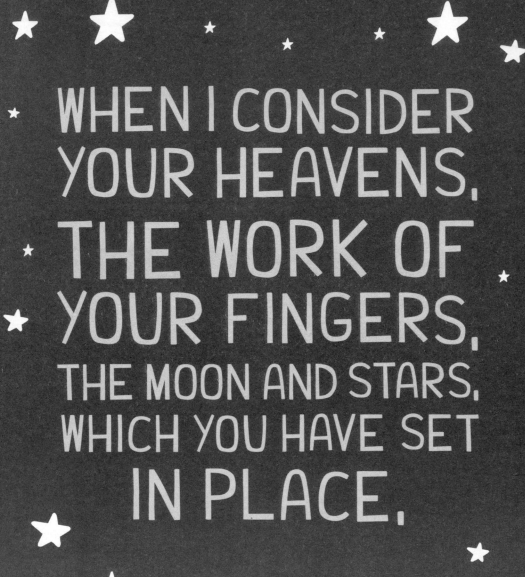

WHEN I CONSIDER YOUR HEAVENS, THE WORK OF YOUR FINGERS, THE MOON AND STARS, WHICH YOU HAVE SET IN PLACE.

WHAT IS MANKIND THAT YOU ARE MINDFUL OF THEM, HUMAN BEINGS THAT YOU CARE FOR THEM?

PSALM 8:3-4

A NOTE FROM THE FARADAY INSTITUTE ABOUT GOD, SCIENCE AND THIS COSMIC COOKBOOK

As humans, we love to question, explore, and discover the world around us, and our place in it. *God's Cosmic Cookbook* uses God's voice to give an overview of mainstream scientific ideas about how the universe works and where everything came from, delighting in the wonder that can grow as we learn ever more about all that God has done.

Sometimes people worry that the scientific discoveries we make might conflict with ideas in the Bible, or that, as more scientific discoveries get made, they might replace our ideas about God. But for many people who believe in God, the more amazing scientific discoveries are made, the more amazed they are about the God they think is behind it all. That's because lots of Christians think of the Bible as a collection of books that help us learn about **who** God is, what he has done, about his relationship with humans and everything else he has made, and what that means for each of us; and they think of science as a way to learn more about **how** God made everything. So, they see science and faith adding to their understanding about God in different ways.

As you can imagine, there are challenges involved in writing a book from God's all-knowing perspective, when we ourselves are humans, and therefore limited by our ever-changing levels of scientific and theological understanding. We simply hope that *God's Cosmic Cookbook* will encourage you and your children to explore this incredible universe, and experience moments of awe and wonder for yourselves, perhaps even sparking your own conversations about the mysterious ways in which God may have worked, and may continue to work unceasingly in the universe around us.

To explore further, check out our other books or head to our website: **www.faradaykids.com**.

ABOUT THE FARADAY INSTITUTE

The Faraday Institute is an interdisciplinary research and communication enterprise linked to the University of Cambridge. Our Youth and Schools Team are committed to providing high-quality events and resources that encourage young people of all ages and backgrounds to explore their questions about the interactions of science and religious faith in exciting and engaging ways.

The **Faraday Institute** for Science and Religion

HODDER FAITH YOUNG EXPLORERS

Hodder & Stoughton is the UK's leading Christian publisher with a wide range of books from the bestselling authors in the UK and around the world. Having published Bibles and Christian books for more than 150 years, Hodder & Stoughton are delighted to launch Hodder Faith Young Explorers – a list of books for children.

Join us on this new adventure!

Visit **www.hodderfaithyoungexplorers.co.uk** to find out more.